MY FAMILY REMEMBERS

The 1990s

James Nixon

W

FRANKLIN WATTS

LONDON • SYDNEY

First published in 2011 by
Franklin Watts
338 Euston Road, London NW1 3BH

Franklin Watts Australia
Level 17/207 Kent Street, Sydney NSW 2000

ISBN: 978 1 4451 0106 4

Dewey classification number: 941'.0859

A CIP catalogue record for this publication is available from the British Library.

Planned and produced by Discovery Books Ltd., 2 College Street,
Ludlow, Shropshire, SY8 1AN
www.discoverybooks.net
Editor: James Nixon
Design: Blink Media

Photo credits: Andy Williams: p. 10 bottom; Bobby Humphrey: p. 30; Canon Inc.: p. 9 bottom-right; Center Parcs: p. 29 bottom-left; Chris Fairclough: pp. 6 bottom, 23 top; Corbis: p. 27 bottom (Yves Forestier/Sygma); Eidos Interactive: p. 14 bottom; Ford Motor Company: p. 27 top; Getty Images: pp. 8 top (Toru Yamanaka/AFP), 20 top (Jacopo Pandolfi), 22 top (Lara Jo Regan), 28 (Cindy Karp/Time & Life Images); Matthew Nixon: p. 13 bottom-right; Melanie Nixon: pp. 13 top, 21 bottom-left; Philips Electronics: pp. 7 right, 9 middle; Psion PLC: pp. 24 top, 25 top; Rex Features: pp. 6 top (Tim Rooke/Nils Jorgensen), 12 top (Nils Jorgensen), 13 middle (SNAP), 16 (SNAP), 18 top (Roger Sargent), 19 middle (Brian Rasic); Shutterstock: pp. 7 top, 9 bottom, 10 top (Jaimie Duplass), 24 bottom (Arvind Balaraman), 27 left; Visa International: p. 11 bottom; Wikimedia: pp. 14 top (Evan-Amos), 15 top-left, 15 top-middle (Tomasz Sienicki), 15 right, 20 middle, 25 bottom, 26 top, 26 middle (Thomas Doerfer); www.picturethepast.org. uk: pp. 8 bottom (Courtesy of George L Roberts), 11 top (Courtesy of Ian Brown/LRPS), 23 bottom (Image Copyright © Nottingham Evening Post).

Cover photos: Getty Images: left (Toru Yamanaka/AFP), right (Peter Still/Redferns).

Words that are bold in the text are explained in the glossary.

Printed in China

Franklin Watts is a division of Hachette Children's Books, an Hachette UK Company.
www.hachette.co.uk

Contents

 Downloadable activity and information sheets
are available at www.franklinwatts.co.uk

Meet the families

The 1990s was a decade of huge changes in technology. Many things that are familiar to us today started in the '90s. Computer networks and the World Wide Web were just beginning. It was the decade of the first digital cameras and DVDs, and mobile phones became widespread. Four children's families share their memories of those days.

Alice

Alice's family

Alice Hibberd is 13 years old. She has an older sister called Meg and lives with her mother, Julie, and stepfather, Tony. Alice has an older stepsister, Lisa, who was in her teens and twenties during the '90s.

Lisa

Sarah

Sarah's family

Sarah Hadland is 12 years old and lives with her older brother, Jacob, and parents, Marcia and Dan. Sarah also has a half brother called James who was aged between 4 and 13 in the '90s.

James

Marcia

Matty

Hazel

Matty's family

Matty Morris is 12 years old. He lives with his younger sister, Milly, his older brother, Peter, and his parents, Julie and Kevin. Julie and Kevin were in their twenties in the 1990s and got married in 1995.

Hazel's family

Hazel Stancliffe is 11 years old. She lives with her older sister, Lily, and her parents, Abigail and Paul. Pippa is one of Lily's older cousins and she was a teenager in the 1990s.

Julie

Pippa

Here is a picture of Matty's parents on their wedding day in 1995.

The feel-good '90s

In the 1990s, there was a growing feeling of hope and **optimism** among people. In 1997, a new government was **elected**, which promised to make life better.

The new, young prime minister, Tony Blair, celebrates his **landslide** election victory in 1997. Blair became associated with 'Cool Britannia'.

The '90s was also an exciting time to be young. People felt proud of Britain. British music and film was successful at home and abroad, and the term 'Cool Britannia' was often used. There was also new technology available that had never been seen before.

Computers began to have a huge impact on people's lives. In 1995, the Microsoft company launched Windows 95, which made it much easier for users to control and operate their machines. The World Wide Web could be used by the public for the first time in 1991. As computers gradually became faster, more and more people began to explore the world of the Web.

The home computer became a common household appliance in the 1990s.

Sarah asks her brother about the Internet in the '90s:
Surfing the Internet became my new favourite hobby. But in the early days it was quite frustrating. Each page would slowly reveal itself bit by bit. There were no flashing images that moved about or jumped out at you – the web pages were static and very simple.

The number of digital gadgets increased during the decade. Digital is the system of carrying information, such as sounds and images, that is used in computers. The technology was also used in the new digital cameras, DVDs and mobile phones.

Computers started to come with CD drives for loading music, pictures and games. Later on, there were DVDs.

In 1997, mobile phones were rarely seen. By the end of the decade they had become an everyday part of life – like they are today.

'I made sure I never left the house without it.'

Alice asks her stepsister about her first mobile phone:
I didn't own a mobile phone until 1999 – I thought I would never need one! In the end I decided I'd better get one in case of an emergency. However, once I had my mobile phone I started using it all the time, and I made sure I never left the house without it!

TIME DIFFERENCE

The number of 15-24-year-olds with a mobile phone jumped from 10 per cent in 1997 to 60 per cent at the end of 1999. Now it is almost 100 per cent!

New technology

In the 1990s, almost everybody could afford the new technology. Computers, their accessories and other gadgets got cheaper and cheaper as the decade went on.

Computers also became a lot more suited for the home. Before the '90s, computers were quite big and unattractive. In 1998, Apple launched its iMacs, which were fun and colourful.

iMac computers came in a range of bright colours.

TIME DIFFERENCE

The number of households with home computers rose from 20 per cent in 1990 to nearly 50 per cent in 2000. Now it is around 75 per cent.

Sky television was available from 1990 and was very popular. It gave families who were willing to pay, lots of extra channels to watch. **Satellite dishes** started to spring up on homes across the country.

'We only had four channels.'

Matty asks her mum about new technology:
Some of my friends had satellite TV in the early '90s and I used to go around to their house to watch it. I couldn't believe the number of channels they had. It was too expensive for my family – we only had four channels.

Satellite dishes in the early '90s were white and stood out much more than they do today.

For much of the '90s, people listened to music and watched videos on **cassette tapes**. But CDs gradually replaced tapes, and in 1995 the DVD (Digital Video Disc) was invented. Films watched on DVD players had a much better picture than those on videotape. On old video recorders you had to wind tape backwards and forwards if you wanted to fast forward or rewind. Doing this lots of times could ruin the tape!

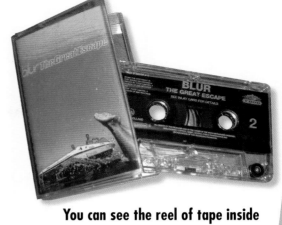

You can see the reel of tape inside this music cassette.

DVD players came on to the market in the late '90s.

Sarah asks her brother about cassette tapes:
I used to record songs off the radio on to cassette tapes and listen to them on my stereo player, which had a tape deck at the front. The sound wasn't too good though. Between each song you could hear the muffled noise of the tape running.

The digital cameras that we use today, went on sale for the first time in 1997. Before then, people used cameras that took photographs on film. To see the pictures, you had to take the film into a shop to be developed.

An early digital camera from 1998.

Once a picture had been taken on a camera with film you could not delete it.

Going shopping

There were big changes in the way we shopped in the 1990s. The Internet and television gave people the chance to shop without leaving the house. More people owned a **debit card** and this made it easy to pay for goods from home.

Among the large number of satellite TV channels were shopping channels trying to sell products. Customers could phone up and order the goods from their living room (right).

As the decade went on, more high street stores and other businesses began to sell their goods on websites. Amazon was launched in 1995 as a book-selling website. Town centres were also losing customers to new out-of-town shopping centres.

'It was very exciting – it had huge shops inside.'

Sarah asks her mum about shops in the '90s: I lived in Birmingham in the '90s and I remember making trips with my sister-in-law to the Merry Hill shopping centre out of town. It was very exciting – it had huge shops inside and had all the big names. Debenhams was my favourite.

The Merry Hill shopping centre outside Birmingham expanded in the 1990s. A monorail was in operation between 1991 and 1996 to transport people from the car parks to the shopping centre.

Trolley Park

Many small local shops had to close down as large **chain stores** and supermarkets could sell things cheaper.

Superstores were built on the edge of town because there was more space and the land was cheap.

Matty asks his mum where she shopped:
I remember when the new Morrisons supermarket was built on the edge of my local town. For me it was great and really easy. The parking was free and there was a **crèche** inside to look after my baby while I shopped.

Stores began to open for much longer in the '90s – some for 24 hours a day. In 1994, the law was changed to allow big shops to open on a Sunday, for six hours.

Since 1994, supermarkets have been allowed to open on a Sunday.

Leisure time

The 1990s gave people a choice of TV programmes to watch like never before. Sky offered channels that showed movies, news or cartoons all day!

Sales of Sky rocketed when they started showing live Premier League football in 1992. It showed other sports, too. Wrestling had stars such as Hulk Hogan and was hugely popular with young boys.

Hulk Hogan enters the ring in 1991 wearing a championship belt around his waist.

American TV had great success in the UK in the '90s. The hit comedy series *Friends* started in 1994 and ran for ten years.

Matty asks his mum what programmes she liked:
I thought *Friends* was hilarious – especially the early series. We had the whole box set on video cassette tapes (left), which we still have!

'I thought *Friends* was hilarious.'

The *Simpsons* cartoon was a big favourite and was popular with adults as well as children. Science fiction drama *The X-Files* and hospital drama *ER* were other big hits.

A girl shows off her Bart Simpson birthday cake. Bart was one of the most popular TV characters of the 1990s.

Alice asks her stepsister about her favourite TV programmes:
I loved series like *ER* and *X-Files*. I was really sad when the handsome Dr Doug Ross played by George Clooney left *ER*. *The X-Files* was about alien investigations. I used to watch it every week with my friends. We would settle down and turn the lights off so we would be even more scared.

In *The X-Files*, agents Fox Mulder (left) and Dana Scully (right) uncover the truth about aliens.

Some people wanted to enjoy their spare time away from a screen. Mountain biking became a popular hobby and a chance to enjoy the outdoors. In the book world, the *Goosebumps* horror series written by R L Stine was a huge hit.

In the 1990s, mountain biking moved from a little-known sport to a popular activity.

Video games and crazes

The Sony Playstation had two ports for a controller and a memory card.

The video games industry took off in the 1990s as the technology improved. The way games looked changed dramatically, from blocky pixels to amazing 3D graphics.

First there were the Sega Mega Drive and Super Nintendo consoles, which used game **cartridges**. Then, in 1995, the Sony Playstation was launched and took gaming to a new level. CDs were used that could store more information than cartridges. Games had 3D worlds to explore and data could be saved on to a memory card.

The Playstation introduced classic titles which we still play today, such as *Gran Turismo, Tekken* and *Tomb Raider*.

Tomb Raider's adventurer Lara Croft became one of the most famous video game characters of all time.

Sarah asks her brother about video games:
In the early '90s, you could not save your video games so you had to play for hours at a time! I used to leave my Nintendo on overnight so I didn't lose my progress. Sometimes I would wake up in the morning and find the game had crashed and then I would have to go all the way back to the start!

Tamagotchi

In 1997, the Tamagotchi became a big craze. It was a tiny computer containing a pet, which you had to look after. If you forgot to feed it for a while it died. The Furby in 1998 was an even more spectacular virtual pet that learned to talk as it grew up!

Furby

Other fads of the '90s included Magic Eye pictures, where you had to find images in a coloured pattern, and Pogs, a game in which you had to win and collect small discs with different pictures.

Magic Eye patterns contained a hidden image. They were a big craze in the mid-'90s.

Slammer

In Pogs, the object of the game was to turn over as many discs as possible, by throwing your 'slammer' disc down on to them.

Alice asks her stepsister about crazes in the '90s:
I remember Magic Eye pictures everywhere at one point – in shops, newspapers and books. I used to spend hours trying to find the hidden picture and it would hurt my head and make me go cross-eyed!

At the movies

Films in the 1990s used jaw-dropping effects in ways never seen before. The amazing *Jurassic Park* (1993) used **computer-generated imagery (CGI)** to make the dinosaurs look very real and terrifying.

Toy Story (1995) was the first film to be completely generated by a computer.

TIME DIFFERENCE

Computer-generated imagery (CGI) was expensive. The average amount of money spent on a film's special effects rose from $5 million in 1995 to $30 million by the end of the decade.

Video recorders were used in the '90s until DVDs took over. People could rent films from a video shop. *Twister* (1996), the story of a large, destructive tornado was another film with stunning CGI. In 1997, it was the first ever film to be released on DVD.

Disney's animations of classic stories were extremely popular in the 1990s, such as *Beauty and the Beast* (1991) and *The Lion King* (1994).

'I loved the songs and watched them over and over again'

The film with the biggest impact of the decade was *Titanic* (1997). It was based on the true story of the SS *Titanic* that crashed into an iceberg and sank in 1912. Millions of people watched it, and the film won 11 **Oscars**!

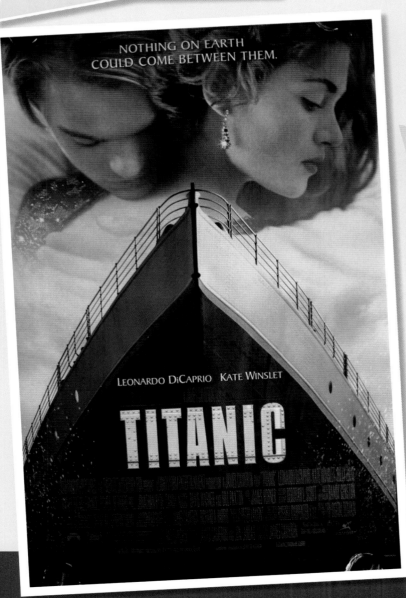

NOTHING ON EARTH COULD COME BETWEEN THEM.

LEONARDO DiCAPRIO   KATE WINSLET

TITANIC

At the time, *Titanic* was the most expensive film ever made.

At the start of the '90s music started to move away from the electronic pop of the '80s to more traditional guitar music.

Grunge was a new style of heavy rock music. The music was quite dark and it was popular with many young people who felt unhappy about the world they lived in. The biggest name in grunge was Kurt Cobain, lead singer of Nirvana. Fans were shocked when he shot and killed himself in 1994.

Kurt Cobain performs live in 1993, a year before his death.

By the mid-'90s rock music had cheered up a bit. There was a wave of popular British bands, such as Oasis, Blur and Pulp. Their music became known as **'Britpop'**.

Oasis' debut album *Definitely Maybe* went straight to number one in the album charts in 1994.

Alice asks her stepsister what music she liked:

I followed the grunge scene in the early '90s, which meant I wore shabby clothes and had very long hair. But my favourite music was Britpop and I saw all the bands. I remember seeing Blur at a big concert in Birmingham. At the end it took us hours to get out of the car park, and I was sure the band sped past us in a blacked-out limo!

This university photo shows Alice's stepsister with long, shaggy hair.

The '90s was also the decade that brought us boy bands. Take That shot to fame in 1992 with their hit single *It Only Takes a Minute*. Other boy bands followed, such as East 17 and Westlife. Girls' hearts were broken in 1996 when Take That split up. Today the band is back together again.

Pop music aimed at teens dominated the charts in the late '90s. The Spice Girls arrived in 1996 with their slogan 'Girl Power'.

Each member of the Spice Girls had a different look – there was (from left to right) 'Posh', 'Baby', 'Scary', 'Ginger' and 'Sporty'.

Hazel asks her cousin if she liked the Spice Girls:

I was not a real fan of the Spice Girls, but me and my friends did dress up as them for a fancy dress party. We all had to decide which one we would each be. I ended up dressing as 'Ginger Spice'.

'I ended up dressing as 'Ginger Spice'.'

In fashion

Compared to the glamour of the 1980s, clothes in the 1990s tended to be more casual, comfortable and plain.

The grunge movement was actually anti-fashion. This scruffy, baggy look was popular among students. Military clothing, such as combat boots and camouflage trousers, was popular in the early '90s and part of the grunge style.

These boots called Doc Martens were the height of fashion in the early '90s.

Baggy clothes remained popular with teenagers until the end of the '90s.

Rebellious teens started a trend for having tattoos and body piercings in lips, tongues and tummies. Piercings and tattoos are more common today and do not shock in the same way as they did then.

Hazel's cousin (left) and her friend dressed up for a party.

Hazel asks her cousin about '90s fashion:
I got a tattoo in 1998 at the same time as my friend got her tongue pierced. She was sick everywhere and couldn't eat or speak properly for two weeks. But, she still managed to hide it from her parents!

For most people, everyday wear was a simple blue jeans and top. Girls sometimes wore crop tops to show their pierced belly button. Band t-shirts were popular to show the music you liked. Hairstyles were simple, too. The straight, layered hair worn by Rachel in the TV hit *Friends* was copied by women all over the world.

Matty asks his mum about hairstyles:
I tried to go for the Rachel look in the '90s, but I don't think I ever quite achieved it. Later on I gave up and went back to having short hair because it was much easier!

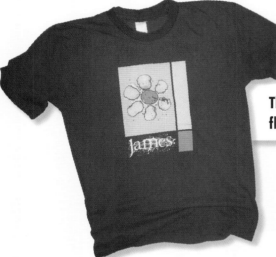

The rock band James released t-shirts with big flowers on the front and girls loved them.

Sportswear was a trend of the '80s that did continue in the '90s. Trainers, tracksuit bottoms and sweatshirts were comfortable and fashionable. But it was important to be seen wearing the correct **brand** name.

Sarah asks her brother about the clothes he wore:
The first thing people would spot on your clothes was the name on it. Even your school shoes had to have a good label, such as Kickers. I remember being very cross when my mum bought me the wrong kind of trainers!

Sports clothing was popular with teenage boys.

Sarah's brother puts on a pair of his trainers.

Schooldays

In the 1990s, the government started to spend more money on schools. Old schools were knocked down and rebuilt, and classrooms were **modernised**. Whiteboards gradually replaced blackboards and there were now computers in most classrooms.

The teacher helps pupils use the computers in an IT lesson in 1997.

A computer room was built into most schools. Regular IT lessons were introduced for the first time as children had new skills to learn.

'I remember sending my first ever email at school.'

Sarah asks her brother about his memories of school:

I remember sending my first ever email on a computer at school. We had to write to a chocolate factory to say we were learning about the company and asked if they could send us any information. I was very happy because they ended up sending me a chocolate Advent calendar!

Sarah's brother about to set off for school.

The amount of tests pupils had to take increased, By the end of the 1990s there were Standard Assessment Tests for 7, 11 and 14 year olds. Maths and English were taught more than other subjects. In 1997, literacy and numeracy hours were introduced into primary schools, which meant an hour of each every day!

In the '90s, more children were encouraged to go on to university after school and college. To cope with the growing numbers of students, universities started to charge **tuition fees** in 1998.

A primary school class sit down and listen to the teacher during their literacy hour.

The Queen visits the student flats at Nottingham University in 1999. More young people were leaving home to go to university in the late '90s.

Hazel asks her cousin about her schooldays: I think my school was a bit old fashioned. We still had a blackboard and no computers in my classroom when I left school in 1995. When I went to university I was in the first group of students that had to pay tuition fees, which was very frustrating.

At work

There were big changes in the workplace in the 1990s. The development of the Internet had the largest impact.

The Internet let people share information across the world in an instant. People could swap files from computer to computer, rather than waiting for days for things to arrive in the post. Emails meant workers spent a lot less time talking on the phone than in the past.

Before email and the Internet, office workers spent much more time talking on the phone.

'There was only one computer that had the Internet.'

Hazel asks her cousin about the computers at work:

I remember doing some work experience at a bank in 1995. There was only one computer that had the Internet! If you wanted to use it you had to book the time you wanted to spend on it in advance.

It became easier for people to work on the move in the '90s. First there were small devices called **pagers**, which could receive short messages. In the early '90s, mobile phones were larger and the reception was often poor. As mobile phone technology improved, more phone masts were built and pagers became less important.

Pager

Personal digital organisers that fitted into the palm of your hand were popular with workers. They could browse the web and allowed you to send and receive emails. They also had extra functions such as an address book and calendar. They were an early form of the smartphones we have today.

Two workers carry their personal digital organisers in the late '90s.

TIME DIFFERENCE

By the end of the 1990s the number of Internet users in the UK had risen to 15 million. Now it is 51.5 million!

The laptop computer was another gadget that helped people work as they travelled. They became common in the 1990s.

Matty asks his mum what changed at work:

I remember my boss buying me a laptop in about 1998. It was quite heavy, but I could use it on the go. It also meant I could work from home and it saved me having to travel 50 miles (80 km) a day!

Laptops in the mid-'90s were much chunkier than the laptops and tablet devices we use today.

On the move

Cars of the '90s gradually became a lot curvier than those in the '70s and '80s. This style has continued until today.

This box-shaped Ford Escort stopped being made in 1990. The fashion was for curvier cars in the '90s, like this Toyota below.

Ford produced some of the most successful cars of the '90s, such as the Fiesta, Focus and Mondeo. Japanese cars, such as Toyota, Honda and Nissan also became popular.

Toyota Corolla

Alice asks her stepsister how she travelled:

When I was at university up in York I used to travel there and back on the train carrying everything in black bin bags! When I was at home I borrowed my mum's Fiesta. The first car of my own was a Toyota Corolla. It had a big boot – perfect for taking my surfboard to the beach!

Sarah asks her brother about cars in the '90s:

My mum drove a Fiesta in the early '90s. It was like a square box on wheels. It had no gadgets, such as electric windows. To get the car going in the morning she had to pull out this lever called a **'choke'**.

Safety features on cars, such as airbags, became standard in the '90s. In 1991, a law was passed which meant passengers had to wear a seatbelt in the back as well as the front.

Pollution and traffic jams were a problem as more cars filled up the roads. Many people who lived in cities turned to bikes and scooters to get about. The miniature 'Smart cars' went on sale in 1998. They did not pollute the air as much as other cars.

Airbags built into the front of cars helped save lives in the 1990s.

It was easy to find a parking space with a Smart car!

TIME DIFFERENCE

Deaths on the road dropped from 5,500 in 1990 to 3,500 by 2000.

In 1994, the Channel Tunnel, which connects Britain to France, was opened. Instead of flying or taking the ferry you could now get a high-speed train to Europe. It became the longest undersea tunnel in the world – nearly 40 kilometres underwater!

A train enters the Channel Tunnel for the first time on a test run in 1993.

Going on holiday

In the 1990s, the number of people taking holidays abroad continued to increase. Holidaymakers were getting more adventurous and trying more **exotic** locations.

Holidays to places such as Australia became cheap enough for many ordinary working people. A skiing holiday in the winter became more popular and affordable, too.

TIME DIFFERENCE

The number of holiday trips abroad increased from 31 million in 1990 to 57 million by the end of the decade!

The island of Ibiza near Spain became the top destination for young adults who wanted to party in the evening and soak up the sun during the day. People were made more aware of the dangers of skin cancer from sunbathing too long, so the use of sunscreens increased.

Holidaymakers sunbathe by the pool at the fast-developing and exotic Veradero Beach resort in Cuba, 1991.

Alice asks her stepsister about holidays abroad:

In 1997, I visited America with my boyfriend and family. It was my first ever long-haul flight. I loved the breakfasts that the plane crew provided in a neat little box. Here are some photos of me at Disneyworld in Florida.

Many families still took their holidays in the UK. Center Parcs holiday villages were popular places to stay. They had swimming pools, tennis courts, restaurants and boating lakes on site.

Sarah asks her brother about his holidays:

When I was about 5 we stayed in a caravan by the sea in Dawlish, Devon. We travelled down on the train with friends and family. I remember being bought a plastic ball for playing on the beach. On the journey home I dropped the ball off the train station platform. My nan had to quickly jump down on to the track to get it back – she was so angry with me!

CenterParcs

Sarah's brother eats some chips by the sea on his holiday in Devon.

Find out what your family remembers

Try asking members of your family what they remember about the 1990s. You could ask them the same questions that children in this book have asked and then compare the answers you get. Ask your relatives how they think that life in the '90s was different from today. Get them to talk about their favourite memories or important events of the time. This will help you build up your own picture of life in the 1990s. It will also help you find out more about your family history.

Everybody dreamed of winning the Lottery when it first started. The advertising slogan was 'It could be you' and the logo was a hand with two fingers crossed.

Timeline

1990 The Gulf War begins in Iraq.

1991 The World Wide Web becomes available to the public.

1994 The Channel Tunnel connecting Britain and France opens.
The mobile phone text messaging service is introduced.
The National Lottery is launched.
The first series of US TV comedy *Friends* is aired.

1995 Sony releases the Playstation in the UK.
The Digital Video Disc (DVD) is invented.
Bands Oasis and Blur challenge each other for top spot in the charts in the 'Battle of Britpop'.

1996 Spice Girls enter the pop scene with their hit song *Wannabe*.
England host the Euro 96 football tournament, but lose to Germany in the semi finals on penalties.

1997 The film *Titanic* wins 11 Oscars.
Tony Blair becomes the new prime minister after a landslide election victory.
Princess Diana dies in a car crash in Paris.

1998 Apple introduces the iMac computer.
The Sky television service goes digital.

1999 On New Year's Eve, parties are held across the world to celebrate the end of a century and the new millennium.

Glossary

brand
A name or symbol that marks a product as different from another.

Britpop
British pop music of the mid-'90s that was influenced by guitar bands of the 1960s, such as The Beatles.

cartridge
A plastic container storing video game data, which can be inserted into a computer or console to be played.

cassette tape
A plastic container with tape inside, used for recording or playing sounds and pictures.

chain store
A shop that is found in many different towns and are all owned by the same company.

choke
A valve that reduces the flow of air in an engine. On old cars, drivers had to operate a choke to get the car's engine started.

computer-generated imagery (CGI)
Visual effects in films created using computer software.

crèche
A place where small children are looked after while their parents are busy.

debit card
A small plastic card which transfers money from your bank account electronically when you make a purchase.

elected
Chosen by a public vote.

exotic
Describes places that are unusual and a long distance away.

graphics
Images produced by computers.

landslide
Describes an election victory when the winner has gained a huge majority of the votes.

modernised
Replaced with new methods or equipment.

optimism
A feeling of hopefulness about the future.

Oscar
The nickname for the small gold statue given as an Academy award. Every year Academy awards are presented for achievements in film.

pager
A small radio device which bleeps to inform the user that they have received a short text message.

pixel
A tiny area on a television screen. An image is formed from many pixels joined together.

satellite dish
An aerial shaped like a bowl, which can receive television signals from a satellite in space.

tuition fees
The money students have to pay to be taught at university.

Further information

Books:
1990s Electronic Media (20th Century Media), by Steve Parker, Heinemann, 2003
The 1990s (Dates of a Decade), by Anne Rooney, Franklin Watts, 2009
The '80s and '90s: Different Paths (20th Century Music), by Jackie Gaff, Heinemann, 2002
The '80s and '90s: Power Dressing and Sportswear (20th Century Fashion), by Clare Lomas, Heinemann, 2000

Websites
This website has lots of memories from people who grew up in the 1990s
http://news.bbc.co.uk/1/hi/magazine/decades/1990s/
On this site find out what TV, music, films, clothes and toys were big in each year of the 1990s.
http://www.bbc.co.uk/cult/ilove/years/90sindex.shtml
For an overview of the 1990s with links to other websites, try
http://www.woodlands-junior.kent.sch.uk/homework/war/1990s.html

Index

Here are the lists of contents for each title in *My Family Remembers...*

1950s
Meet the families • After the war • Places to live • Going shopping • Life at home
Having fun • Television and film • Sounds of the '50s • Petticoats and Teddy Boys
Schooldays • At work • Getting about • Holiday time • A new beginning

1960s
Meet the families • Exciting changes • Places to live • Going shopping
Life at home • Film and television • Having fun • The decade of Pop
Fashion • At work • Schooldays • Getting about • Holiday time

1970s
Meet the families • Gloom and glitter • Life at home • Going shopping • Playtime
At the movies • Leisure time • From glam rock to punk • Fashions • Schooldays
At work • Getting about • Holiday time

1980s
Meet the families • A changing world • Life at home • Going shopping • Leisure time
Toys and crazes • Watching films • Sounds of the '80s • Power dressing to sportswear
Schooldays • At work • Getting about • Holiday time

1990s
Meet the families • The high-tech '90s • New technology • Going shopping
Leisure time • Video games and crazes • At the movies • Pop music
In fashion • Schooldays • At work • On the move • Going on holiday

2000s
Meet the families • The noughties • Technology at home • At work
Going shopping • Entertainment • Video gaming • On film • From CDs to iPods
In fashion • Schooldays • Travelling • Holidays